GW00771699

Dr. Katrin Luzar

THE CONFIDENCE COMMANDMENTS

Make confidence your superpower!
Ten strategies
from women for women.

With special support from Maren Hallin,
Natascha Hoffner, Larraine Solomon, Katharina Schulze,
Roxanne Tashjian, Claudine Petit, Elke Guhl,
Roxana Hughes, Lou Goodman

THE CONFIDENCE COMMANDMENTS. Copyright ©2021 by Katrin Luzar. All rights reserved. Printed in Germany. No part of this book may be used or reproduced in any manner whatsoever without written permission.

www.confidence-commandments.com
info@confidence-commandments.com
First edition

Publishing House and Print:
tredition GmbH, Halenreie 40-44, 22359 Hamburg

Cover Design by:
Fiaz Ahmed Ifran, https://99designs.com/profiles/1735673

ISBN
Paperback   978-3-347-29625-1
Hardcover   978-3-347-29626-8
e-Book   978-3-347-29627-5

CONTENTS

Nice to meet you

Introduction

Hello! I want to start this book by saying: You have a superpower.

Perhaps you didn't know that. My goal is to unleash that superpower together with you. You will work on your confidence and discover ten strategies and principles that will help you develop your self-esteem day by day. You are not alone. You will get support from women who have faced the confidence challenge themselves. They are in your corner during the journey and are called Maren, Lou, Roxanne, Larraine, Natascha, Elke, Roxana, Claudine, and Katharina. They will share their personal stories and recommendations with you. You will see that confidence is nothing that is unachievable. Yes, it might take some effort. Nevertheless, I am a strong believer that confidence is like a muscle we can train, and this is your workbook.

But let's start at the beginning. This project began with a post on LinkedIn. In the spring of 2020 – the pandemic had just started – I asked some women in my network what they did as team leaders to make sure the women in their teams felt confident and empowered to speak up, raise their hand, and have an opinion. The feedback was overwhelming. I received so many great tips that it got me thinking. Wouldn't it be helpful to put all these real-life examples and proven concepts together in one place and share it? It would've been such a loss not to do something with it.

Confidence is a matter that is truly dear to my heart. I first came in touch with it in a professional manner due to a series of projects my team at Monster.com did approximately three years ago. And after that, the topic remained a constant in my life. We wanted to encourage young women and girls to look into a career in coding. Also, we did several surveys about the confidence level of women in the workplace. It was surprising that it is not the lack of know-how or expertise that hinders women, including me, to have a career or take the next step. It is the lack of self-esteem. I started to do research on the origin of confidence, the different aspects and levels of confidence, and how you can strengthen it. I interviewed a lot of women because I was wondering if it was only me who was struggling with self-esteem. And found that I was not alone, not at all. Nearly all of them had stories and examples of confidence failures. It was a great relief on the one hand. It wasn't just me. But on the other hand, it revealed that it is much bigger issue and a massive concern for virtually every woman. The next question had to be: What can we do to solve it? We cannot accept that women are missing out on job and career opportunities because of a lack of confidence. Something had to be done.

My first milestone was the creation of the Confidence Blocklist. You can find it at the end of this book. It was the warm-up exercise for my own confidence training. I wanted to create something that reminds me to work on my self-esteem every day as, obviously, I also experienced long periods of low self-esteem and self-doubt at school, at university, and at my first jobs. The Confidence Blocklist is a handy tool. But I didn't want to stop there.

From women for women! The Confidence Commandments mark the next step. Like any good list of commandments, there are ten. Based on the reaction on LinkedIn, I reached out to my network and connected each of the ten commandments with one female expert. Every commandment has its roots in a project, a conversation, or an experience I had with Elke, Sinead, Roxana, Lou, Larraine, Roxanne, Claudine, Maren, or Natascha. You will meet them in a second. They will share their personal stories with you. I am very thankful that they have been so open and honest. This way, you not only have tips, but you can see how they work in real life. As Katharina Schulze, a true feminist, says at the end of this book: "You have everything you need in yourself – and you will learn the rest on your journey." If you like, jump quickly to the last chapter and read what she has to say to you. I find her statement most encouraging and motivating.

The commandments are my personal selection – no guarantee for completeness. I hope they will cover some of the most relevant areas that you encounter in your business life: competition, unfair bosses, the fear to speak in meetings or on stage, the feeling of being alone or overwhelmed, and having problems with accepting a praise. I will introduce each commandment briefly, share the context and will then hand over to the experts! I took over two commandments myself as they are very important to me personally.

Make Confidence your superpower. Just test the tips from the book. Some might be easier or more applicable to you. Take your time and select what suits your individual journey the best. The confidence experts believe in you. You can do it.

And to make sure that you will be able to enjoy your newly found self-esteem superpower, your confidence team have added a bonus commandment: Don't be scared of success.

THE CONFIDENCE COMMANDMENTS

1. **Find a wingwoman (could be a man)**
   Katrin Luzar
2. **Plan for small-step victories**
   Roxana Hughes
3. **Do not compare compulsively**
   Katrin Luzar
4. **Done is better than perfect**
   Claudine Petit
5. **Formulate statements, not questions**
   Elke Guhl
6. **Eliminate distractions and do not hide behind them**
   Roxanne Tashjian
7. **Use the power of 'no'**
   Lou Goodman
8. **Be confident on the outside and you will also become it on the inside**
   Larraine Solomon
9. **Accept compliments and give them to others often**
   Maren Hallin
10. **Make it about others**
    Natascha Hoffner

Bonus: Don't be scared of success

1. Find a wingwoman (could be a man)

I was in the audience when my manager at that time, Sinead, pulled up a slide and introduced the concept of the wingwoman to the listeners at the German event herCareer. It got amazing feedback, as it was something many women seemed to not have thought about before. I was personally touched as she presented my colleague Maren and myself as wingwomen examples from her professional life. What an honor. The idea of not being alone in situations when you struggle with your confidence is so great. That is why I will explain it to you.

Finding yourself a wingwoman is the first thing to do when you start on your confidence journey.

After you read this chapter, take some minutes to do a quick brainstorm: Who has been supportive in your past? Who always makes you smile? Who gives you constructive feedback that really helps, opens new perspectives, and takes you to the next level? These humans are all wingwoman candidates.

The term wingwoman is new, you mostly read about wingmen. This is a military term. In the Air Force, the wingman is a pilot who supports and helps another pilot in battles. The term gained inglorious fame in the last century after it was used in movies, like Top Gun, or in TV series and stands for a man who helps another man to approach potential female partners. "I'll take you under my wing" – in a bar, this means your wingman is cheering you on, playing dumb to let you shine, or is getting into a conversation of the beautiful lady's best friend to give you more exclusivity with her while flirting like hell. Going into "battle" together can lead to a more successful outcome. And I assume that you all have some experience with these two-man teams approaching you and your friends while you are just trying to enjoy a quiet round of cocktails.

But besides the fact that wingmen can be annoying, the concept is a winner. It is just better to tackle difficult situation in pairs. And what is true for the private life is also true for the professional life.

In business, a partner can help you:

- to not feel alone
- to have someone to look at during speeches
- to have someone who always applauds and laughs first

Bringing a wingwoman to a meeting is gold. While you give your presentation, she is the one reading the room. You can make eye contact with her regularly, and she can send signals like move on, be louder, you are doing great, not so fast, etc. She is giving you the confidence that you are doing ok.

Your wingwoman is also the one who verbally supports you. Most of you might have been in a meeting situation where you suggested a particular strategy and then ten minutes later, a colleague (most likely a man) suggests the same and starts to sell your idea as his own. While you are still shocked about this total impudence, your wingwoman will take care of it: "This is exactly Emily's idea from before the coffee break. I think we should ask her to repeat it again."

Also, the wingwoman is always there to promote your idea: "Correct, Emily. I am supporting your idea. Thank you." This way, you will never experience dead silence after you have plucked up your courage and spoken your mind.

"SURE, AND CAN YOU BE MINE?"

To make this a success, your wingwoman needs to know that she is your wingwoman and needs a briefing. This might be your first hurdle. Don't be shy to ask another woman to help you out. You will find that after you have gotten past the first explanation, the woman in front of you will just say, "Sure, and can you be mine?" We are all longing for a wingwoman.

Then you must provide a briefing. Explain what the speech, the presentation, the small talk, networking event is about, what you would like to achieve, what you fear the most, and what good support for you could look like. It should not feel weird, and the wingwoman should not bring pompoms and a megaphone. Agree on subtle strategies. Your wingwoman is your rock in stormy waters.

Personally, I actively offer colleagues to be their wingwoman. I know that some are too shy or have not even thought about that option. In my position as Communications and Marketing Director, I often organize events and larger meetings. If I spot that one of the participants is nervous before going to the microphone, I just go and say where I will sit or stand.

The colleague should make regular eye contact with me, and I will signal to her how it is going by nodding, smiling, gesturing to my wristwatch for time, or giving a thumbs up. Very often, the colleague is instantly more relaxed, and you can see the relief that she is not alone. Also, I am the first to applaud! Very important to get the crowd going. When appropriate, I also offer to give feedback. This way, the colleague is getting a direct review, can ask questions, and together, we can look at what could be changed for next time to be even better.

Just try it. This concept is a life changer. Women need to lift each other up!

For me, learning about the wingwoman concept was one of the most powerful experiences in my life. And I must thank my former manager Sinead for it.

Oh – before I forget: Your wingwoman can also be a man.

2. Plan for small-step victories

*Years ago, I was hiring to fill a position in my team; that was when I first came across **Roxana "Roxy" Hughes**. Roxy came from an interesting professional background, and you could say that her CV was a patchwork of many pieces. It demonstrated diversity from many angles, from cultures she had experienced, to the types of companies she had worked for, and the variety of positions she had held. Some would have described her as a job hopper, but there was far more to it. I was intrigued, and my curiosity paid off when I hired her. From the beginning of Roxy's time in my team, she had not only a knack of seeing the bigger picture but also an ability to focus on the relevant parts and problems of a project that needed to be addressed in order to achieve our various goals. Curious, confident, and bright, Roxy was observant with a strong work ethic, and when the time came around to write the confidence commandments, I knew right away that it was her I had to contact.*

So, Roxana, as someone who's able to identify the small steps and not become overwhelmed by the larger project, what can you share that will help other professionals?

Well, as a young girl, I could have been described by my teachers and parents as overconfident... perhaps even boisterous! But that is only a tiny part of my story. It's easy to be confident in situations that you are familiar with: at home, with friends, in school, for example. Because I changed schools regularly growing up, though, I was faced with constant change, unfamiliar surroundings, and new challenges. This left me shy and introspective. I spent a lot of time alone, minding my own business, and this meant it was tough for me to make new friends.

This part of my story is not so unique, perhaps you and I even have this in common. Are you the party leader amongst your friends? The organizer? That's me. It took time for me to grow my professional confidence. When I was younger and was faced with senior bosses or managers, I found it hard to overcome the challenge of being overlooked or ignored about subjects that I had studied, experienced or, heck, even had degrees in. It was hard to navigate the tricky waters of going against the company norm or working out how to challenge that one boss who "doesn't get it" and to feel heard and validated. If you have experienced this, too, then maybe we are more similar than you think.

Gaining confidence was a journey for me and not a God-given talent. BTW, it still is a journey and probably always will be. Being confident is not about knowing all the answers or being the loudest in the room, it's not about ignoring those around you because you think you are right. Being confident is about being comfortable in ambiguity, relaxed in the unknown... knowing you have the resilience, patience, and intelligence to figure it out. It comes from an assuredness, a trust in oneself.

It took me a while to find the best words to write for this chapter. Even now, after the challenges, wins, and defeats in my life, just the process of writing this left me in doubt about my own credibility several times. So, I decided to focus on my own journey, my times in which I felt a crisis of confidence, and to just speak from the heart, about times I had to believe in myself and either faked my confidence or put everything out there despite feeling terrified.

Along the way, I have made mistakes or been too direct, sometimes I have upset the status quo, challenged too many old ways of thinking, even to the point of getting fired… twice! But we will get to that later, because I want you to know, confidence is born not from arrogance but from a constant and patient belief in oneself. Here are some tips for your journey, broken down by each component of my work practice, with two examples from the job…

Example 1 – How a webinar told me about focus

Several years ago, I walked into a marketing team whose main role was to support the sales team. One of the high-profile projects was to turn around an unsuccessful webinar series about the company's products. The first webinars had been unsuccessful, they only had a few participants and, in some instances, no customers at all, only colleagues. It was getting no traction. Sitting in the meetings, I was initially nervous to speak up, because at the time, I had never set up a webinar before. But I had experience from being an active webinar consumer myself. In those days, webinars were still new and exciting. I was young and hungry, so I participated in anything I could register for that could improve my marketing knowledge – this alone put me at somewhat of an advantage compared to my peers. Little side note: Be hungry! Being hungry for knowledge will build up confidence, too.

So, two quick tips. First, focus on what you know and stick to it. I don't mean stick to making coffee and creating photocopies as you might have been stuck with during an internship. Instead, use the stuff you know, what you have learned, what you have experienced, and what you have studied. Being active on social media, being active editing photos, being active watching TED talks can put you at an advantage when compared to someone who does none of those things.

Somehow, I ended up being asked to sit in on one of the review meetings for the next webinar series. Sitting there surrounded by the back and forth of ideas and examinations, by these experienced professionals, I could somehow see and understand right away why the webinars had been unsuccessful thus far. The project team saw the webinars purely as a tool to generate sales, as a platform to present the product specifications. Solely from the standpoint of experiencing many webinars myself, I knew this wasn't how successful webinars were conducted. People don't watch webinars to see product advertisements.

We needed to take the opportunity to change the storyline and entertain/inform our audience. So, after analyzing the content, looking around at my team and based on my gut feeling, I proposed a new webinar series that would do exactly that. In the beginning, as was to be expected, there was NO support from the sales management team. I was confident I could make this work and stuck to my guns, I focused on reworking the webinars together with the team, knowing I was risking my professional reputation – but I would worry about that later. When we began to advertise the reworked webinars, we secured an increase in registrations by over 400%. This proved that my confidence and focus had paid off in this instance.

In the end, although they had to concede that it had been approached wrongly, some colleagues tried to steal much of the limelight for the success. I didn't mind and moved on from it because together, we had improved something and increased value to our customer base. For a while, I was a little bitter about this, but looking back, I can see now how it is important to…

Try not to get lost

Every step you take on a new path can bring doubts, questions, and insecurity. We have a tendency to blow the whole scenario out of proportion and make it bigger than it actually is. If I asked you: How would you eat an elephant? The response is easier than you think. One bite at a time. There is no other way to get through it, is there?

"IF I ASKED YOU: HOW WOULD YOU EAT AN ELEPHANT? THE RESPONSE IS EASIER THAN YOU THINK. ONE BITE AT A TIME."

The haze of doubt and insecurity comes from the stone age, the in-built mental security system. Thousands of years ago, being part of a community or group was essential to our survival, being kicked out or ostracized in those times would have meant certain death. So, our brain wants us to fit in and to not go against the tribe/team/company. Our senses are remnants from another time and haven't adjusted. Most of the time, they hinder us instead of helping us, as we act in mostly safe surroundings.

Don't get lost in that fear: the worry that something could go wrong, someone could misunderstand, you might overstep, and worst of all, you might get fired. After I was let go twice in my life, I can only recommend it. GET FIRED! Life does go on! Don't get lost in unrealistic, self-produced pressure. We live in times where everyone is talking about his or her great achievements, but there is little to no talk about the small steps that have led us there. I absolutely get it! I have been there, too: "I am over 35, I am not successful, I am still not leading a team or running my own company. Something must be wrong with me!" Ambition is fine, but not at the expense of focusing on where you are now and the next steps you need to take in order to achieve your goals so...

Boil it down

Early in the morning, a day before the webinar, the manager of the presenter came over and told me that the presenter would not be available for the webinar the next day. That was the first shock to my system, and it was only nine in the morning. The second shock was being told to reschedule the webinar for another day...

Well, instead of just following the chain of command, I thought about what was truly important to the success of the project. It boiled down to this: A high number of registrations equals a satisfactory number of participants and thereafter additional sales generated. Rescheduling would cost us registrations.

Instead of cancelling, I put forward an idea to evaluate and find someone else to present the webinar. This was not the easy option, but it was the best one. Adjusting the presentation and maintaining quality in that short amount of time was a challenge, but as a team, we were able to do it. It felt amazing to challenge the way the webinar was written and then to challenge the team about who was going to do it and how it was going to be done. But I stuck to my guns and afterwards earned a great deal of respect from my peers for making this project a success. I often reflect that none of this would have happened if I had just done as I was told. Don't forget to...

Celebrate and be proud

I will always remember a few pivotal moments in my career, the aforementioned webinar project, the photo shoot I had to save or, as an intern, when taking over the stalled rejuvenation of a website, where after months of work, others had only published lots of LOREM IPSUMs. Over the years, I have found that it is easy to talk yourself down or forget about things you have achieved. But remembering these smaller victories can give you a boost and build you up and, for some, even let you grow a little taller, so...

Example 2 – How a car taught me to be bold

When I worked at what is perhaps one of the coolest start-ups of the 21st century, Tesla Motors, I did so at a time before anyone really knew of them, back when their first mainstream EV – The Model S – had driven on European roads. I was part of a small team of young, enthusiastic, and well-educated 20-something's who were proud and hungry to help change the automotive industry forever.

The customers – the Tesla reservation holders – shared these feeling as well. In the early days, people were even reserving production spots for their vehicles, without knowing exactly how they could configure their Model S – such was the hype! It was exciting to be a part of these early days, the pace of the day-to-day operation was frenetic, because start-ups need to move faster and be more flexible and less hierarchical. All of that was true for Tesla, who was then at the dawn of a revolution for automotive transportation – the electric revolution. When the time came for people to finally configure their cars, lots of people cancelled their reservation spots because they were missing certain equipment features that they wanted but were showing as unavailable. Internally, we already had the information that these features would be coming soon and that all cars would be built with them as standard. But at that time, we weren't allowed to communicate it.

You can probably imagine, as a young company, it was important for Tesla to keep customers happy and keep reservations in the books in order to consequently sell cars. With the internal knowledge I had, with the orders falling away, I did the boldest move of my career so far.

I directly emailed Elon Musk.

How do you make a rational decision to email the original inspiration for Tony Stark – IRON MAN??

By boiling it down. Of course, I could have talked to our local management, but I knew their answer already. So, I trusted Elon's Words "if you have a problem and you know who to talk to to fix it – Go for it!" So, I did.

My whole body was as tense as a bowling ball, sitting there in our tiny office, feeling the need to be secretive about it, my pulse rising, thinking 'what if…?' What if I get in trouble for it? What if I have gone over my manager's head, and they get pissed at me? What if?? I just clicked the send button and closed my eyes. When I came into the office the next day, starting my computer and opening my email client felt like a century. And there it was. Elon's reply. He was brief and to the point because, well, Elon Musk.

Bottom line is that he gave all of the European team the go-ahead to talk about the upcoming features. As a result, we lost fewer orders, and more Model S vehicles got on the roads earlier. The electric revolution continued. I am not suggesting that you go to work tomorrow and start spamming the CEOs and Managing Directors of your companies. But instead of carefully evaluating a situation, trust your gut and take the next crucial steps towards your bigger goal.

Focus, don't get lost, boil it down, celebrate & be proud, be bold enjoy the ride!

3. Do not compare compulsively

A flower does not think of competing with the flower next to it. It just blooms. What a wonderful quote from the world of yoga. When I look at my personal career, I must admit that the urge to compare myself constantly is my biggest daily challenge. My colleague and HR expert **Claire** *said to me: Do not compare compulsively. It is not good for your confidence. Perhaps it is because I am the twin of a very intelligent and smart sister who never had problems at school and mastered the hardest mathematical problems with ease – she was even the best in Latin at school. A competitor who is hard to beat. To have a sibling exactly your age and development level might trigger an urge to compare whatever you do – pictures, tests... puzzles. So much for private life comparisons. In a job environment, I think comparison is a natural and needed behavior. If you want to produce the best product or service, you must compare your company to others. It is also necessary to thrive personally and to make career steps to develop a healthy attitude towards competition. But what if comparison takes over? When you cannot let go?*

To be clear, comparison and competition are normal human behaviors. Without them, most innovations wouldn't have happened. People you admire today for their courage and exceptional life's work would not come to your mind while thinking "role model" without competition. Most sporting events would only be a lukewarm display of fitness. To be better than someone else can boost your confidence. You might be unsure if you can do the project, be in the spotlight on stage, or get the acknowledgment for your personal work in the team. And then, directly before your speech at the event, the previous speaker delivers a disaster of a presentation. Now you go on stage with the feeling: I can beat that. You do your best and get the applause. In this case, you compare yourself, decide that you are so much better prepared, and you earn the success.

In psychology and sociology, the concepts of comparison and competition have been topics of hundreds of surveys and papers. We cannot go into the theoretical background here. For our purpose, and to raise some attention for the topic in connection with confidence, I would like to talk about three levels of comparison that I have experienced in my career:

1. **Normal** – to check how you are doing
2. **Competitive** – there is someone who I think is better and whom I need to outrun
3. **Compulsive** – comparison no matter what and with the idea that I must be the best of the best, to prove I am worth the compliment or the position

Normal comparison: Let's describe it as a sideward comparison. Examples are trainings or when you find yourself in a new position or a new job. There is nothing wrong with looking at the others to see where you are and if there are things you might learn from your peers. We can also mention salary negotiations as an example. You should absolutely do a comparison between the money you earn and the earnings of your direct peers every other year to make sure you get what you deserve.

Competitive comparison: You can see this often in the form of upward comparisons. It can be with other persons or in business environments and between your company/product and the outside competition. This is normal and, in many positions, you will find a competitive mindset helpful and necessary to thrive in your career. When I advise employees and my team, I always tell them to keep that competitive view, but to stay fair and keep the balance. In my position as team lead, my role is to identify employees or candidates for open positions with the potential to take over larger or more challenging projects. One element in the assessment is to show a healthy degree of competitive mindset. This gives the candidate the necessary confidence to tackle situations that seem extremely hard or even unsolvable. To address a problem with "I don't know, why I shouldn't do it if others can?" will help you to keep your eye on the finish line. Is there something to keep in mind? You should always stay fair. When you see that you are losing against another person or with your business idea, cheating or playing dirty is not the solution. In the end, it is also better for your confidence to win fair and accept that you might need more time or other skills to beat your competition.

"BUT WHEN I CANNOT BE EXTRAORDINAIRE, HOW CAN I BE CONFIDENT?"

Compulsive comparison: You notice it when the comparisons never stop, and you cannot flee the vicious cycle in your head anymore. Let's look at some indicators of compulsive behaviors that will never lead to more confidence, self-acceptance, or self-respect.

A first indicator is to always compare upwards: You pick the most beautiful, most successful, most confident person and start to contrast yourself against her or him. But this will fail. Not everyone can be extraordinary, a millionaire, or a cover girl. This is hopeless and doing it too often damages your confidence and your mental health. "But when I cannot be extraordinaire, how can I be confident?" Your question should not be if you are extra special or not. While being in an upward comparison cycle, your question should be: What am I comparing myself against? Did I pick the right criteria for a comparison? Looks and long legs are hard to compare with if you are born 5 feet 2 inches. And not every successful business personality did it without the help of family, a supporting network, etc. You should take a second to find out under what circumstances the extraordinary people have become who they are and evaluate if your personal situation is similar to that at all, before you get depressed that you will never be the next star in The Wallstreet Journal.

A second indicator is to not be able to stop the process of comparison and include all, even the tiny, aspects of your life. This is hard to change, as comparing ourselves to others is a part of our human behavior, a thought scheme we are all born with. Everyone who has experienced a phase of compulsive comparison knows that it is stressful and costs energy to gain self-affirmation only through thinking that you did something better than others (and even if it is only stocking the fridge the optimal way). You are standing on shaky ground, as something can go wrong any minute. And this fear will weaken the confidence you gained in the first place.

The third indicator is perfectionism. Personally, I do not like the term, and it makes me prick up my ears when candidates or employees are trying to sell perfectionism as a strength. In theory, the goal to do something one hundred percent perfect is good, but perfectionism is rarely achieved. Perfectionism is therefore an attitude that will not help you with your confidence. In case you currently define yourself as a perfectionist, it might be good to take a minute to review what exactly you mean by that and if there are other terms that describe it more accurately. So, what is the resolution for our Confidence Commandment "Do not compare compulsively"? I advise that you bring it to a constructive end. Sometimes it is good to compare your current self to your past self to see your positive change and to be proud of that. You can gain a lot of confidence from your past achievements. On the web, I found this anonymous quote: "Comparison is the best way to judge our progress but not with others, compare your yesterday with your today."

Also, it helps to think the comparison idea through to the end. If you get that top position in your company, will you be happy with the long hours, the pressure, and the political games that often come along with it? If you want to be the fittest 40+ in your city, are you willing to accept the strict diet, the early mornings on the running track, and the sore muscles?

The full comparison includes what you must give up. And it includes what you would gain if you decided against it, too. A better work-life balance, time to read or quality time with family and friends, enjoying a good meal or lots of chocolate, of course! Remember, Theodore Roosevelt said: "Comparison is the thief of joy." Comparison can lead to more confidence when done in healthy doses. But if you do not compare, that is also ok.

4. Done is better than perfect

*I am a perfectionist – sounds familiar? Have you already used this as your "weakness" in a job interview? Yes, me too. I tried to make it sound like a strength hidden in a weakness, but actually, perfectionism is a threat to your confidence. (And, by the way, recruiters are pretty bored by hearing this during an interview.) I fell into the trap of trying to do everything 150 percent, because I thought it was expected, and it did nothing for my confidence. It often stopped me from doing things at all, because I thought I would never be able to manage it perfectly (from my point of view) and that I would be totally embarrassed by trying. But one day it hit me – the philosophy of "done is better than perfect". It is totally unrealistic to be perfect all the time. You just have too much on your plate having a career, being a parent, being a good partner, being the best friend. Let's learn how someone with a lot on her plate made use of the concept during the last 12 months – **Claudine Petit**.*

My name is Claudine Petit, and I am 39 years old. I live in Munich and work as a Lead Corporate Strategy MSD Germany. But let me start at the beginning:

My sign of the zodiac is Virgo, I am a single child and come from a working-class family in the unpretentious federal state of Saarland. In my childhood and youth, I was always average in everything that I did and had to work very hard to be amongst the heads of the pack. I don't even know why

I wanted to be at the front. It was simply an urge deep within me, as I was never pressured by my parents.

But I have always been ambitious and quickly realized that I could make progress through hard work and with my open nature. Thus, my pattern quickly developed: I can do anything as long as I plan and structure it well and work very hard.

Let me explain why I rather believe in the following words today: Done is better than perfect.

My life's philosophy for my "double income, no kids" lifestyle worked well for a while. But I am starting to realize that this can't be everything. At least not for me. The right man was at my side, my work was going well, and as a patchwork mom to my husband's son, I quickly realized that I wanted to be a mother myself. And I realized for the first time that it isn't enough to simply work hard and plan everything because I could work as hard as I wanted but I simply didn't get pregnant. It was frustrating, took a lot of energy, and I no longer had – for the first time in a very, very long time – the feeling that I could achieve everything, that I could be perfect. I lost my belief that everything would work out in the end. I couldn't make it all perfect. Evidently, I couldn't even make it at all. I was powerless.

This was the first lesson of helplessness, one of many that would teach me in the following five years that you can't control and plan everything.

Sometimes, it is so much better to simply do things spontaneously and to live

At some point, I became pregnant. Our daughter was born, and I advanced in my career. Everything seemed to be going well. We wanted another child, but it was difficult once again, hopeless. We tried everything, but without success. However, we didn't give up because, after all, everything else was going so well, and the illusion that "I have everything under control, as long as I work really hard" had long returned to my life. Until I received the diagnosis on October 9, 2019, that I had borderline tumors of the ovary.

Wham! And suddenly, everything came undone, there was no more control, no more plans, no second child, and most certainly no assurance that everything would be okay. I simply found myself in a freefall.

Why am I telling you this now?

Because it was my painful lesson that it makes no sense to go for perfection and for 100% plannability. My definition of perfect was this: give birth to at least two children, have a career, be a wife, be financially independent, be involved in the community, etc. You know what I am talking about, don't you?

"I CAN ACTUALLY HAVE MY OWN DEFINITION OF WHAT 'PERFECT' MEANS TO ME."

I had to learn to let go and to first place one foot in front of the other, to give myself into the hands of the best doctors, and to get better by taking baby steps. I recovered and learned, admittedly with professional help, that everything is "perfect" just the way it is now. Because I can actually have my own definition of what "perfect" means to me. It doesn't always have to be higher, farther, bigger, and better. I learned to live in the here and now. To be content and very grateful.

I define when something is perfect or adequate for me

Part of my here and now, however, also includes a demanding job, the need to see my (patchwork) kids not just on weekends, to be a good mother, a good partner, but also a good friend, a good daughter ... well, all that can sometimes be a bit much.

But what is important to me is that I want to do exactly these things that are associated with them. My doctors sometimes tell me: "Mrs. Petit, take it easy every now and then." But I don't want to take it easy because this is exactly what I enjoy doing. I want to do exactly these things, but I can't do them 150%. Things

34

are left undone, and that is totally okay. I am able to accept this now. I am good at my job, I know that. But I am nowhere near the 150 percent of preparedness that I used to be at. I am often not even prepared at all. But I know my strengths. Years ago, I found a nice definition of (self-)confidence in the Cambridge Dictionary: *Behaving calmly because you have no doubts about your ability or knowledge.*

And that is exactly what this is all about. After years on the job and after several less nice experiences in life, I have become calmer and more satisfied. I am closer to my own true self und know very well what I can do and what I can't. When it is okay to put more energy into something, and when those 80 percent are just enough.

Live confidently with 80 percent

This doesn't mean that you do tasks more poorly that before, no. What I can say about myself is that I am more focused. I delegate more. Do I really have to do everything myself or couldn't someone on my team do it much better?

I say 'no' more frequently now. Whether it is the amazing innovative project from my global colleagues or the third dinner with the management board in a single quarter. Don't get me wrong. Of course, you have to do this every now and then, those are the rules in the world of business when you want to get ahead.

But I can more easily now say: "No, not tonight. I want to be with my kids and tuck them in."

The same also goes for my personal life: Sometimes, I don't have the time to bake another cake for kindergarten. I'll rather bring the prosecco for the summer party. My husband knows that I can't cook and that I don't like to clean. Someone else definitely needs to iron his shirts, unless he only wants to wear them once. We have found solutions for this, too: My husband irons the clothes in our house. In return, I take the kids to bed. Sometimes my husband (who also cooks, in fact) simply wants to sit down for a ready-made meal, in which case I either use the Thermomix or order takeout! But I no longer feel guilty about those things because I am good at other things. And everyone is happy.

I think, however, that this depends on the type of person – we all have to ask ourselves what is important to us. I believe that people can also be happy if they do fewer things in life, but to do those things perfect then. This doesn't work for me because I find too many things so very exciting. And I think I need it, too. On the one hand, my mind needs the distraction, but on the other hand, my heart also needs many different inspirations and gets excited by various things. We have to accept that there simply isn't enough time to complete each task at 150%.

Making choices for yourself is a sign of self-respect

I love sports. I am physically very active, but on a casual level, the way I can incorporate it into my schedule. Sometimes it can be just 30 minutes of jogging or yoga. That has nothing to do with high-performance training. Can I keep up with my super athletic friends who can spontaneously run 28 km? Nope. Another example: I want to be a good and attentive mother. Does that mean that my kids never watch TV, only eat organic, and that I never check my mails while I am actually doing crafts with them? Nope. I have to admit, I would like to, but I simply can't always manage that.

I want to meet the requirements of a demanding job that satisfies me and that pays the bills of my 'good' life. Am I ambitious enough to become even more successful? Yes, definitely. Is it going as fast as I had imagined it to go all those years ago? No, because I can't and don't want to spend all my time on the job anymore.

Since receiving my cancer diagnosis, I have strictly been following a 4-day workweek schedule. I am the first manager in my company to do this. Of course, I also have off days during which I work for a little bit, but never more than three hours, and many of those off days are truly off.

My decisions have also earned me the respect of others – and given me the self-confidence to continue on this path

I should tell you something, however: I don't believe that this has limited my chances to advance in my career. On the contrary. I know that many of my colleagues and superiors value my conscious choice to spend more time on my health and with my family and admire me for it. This results in me doing the really important things with an appropriate time investment. And this leads to success – and I feel great like this.

I also believe that it makes you more likeable when you are imperfect at times. But it is important to communicate this transparently. The new flexible work structures surely provide a great opportunity here.

When a meeting already begins with a 2-minute check-in during which you can say that you are completely exhausted because your child had a fever, or you had to finish the Powerpoint presentation for the management board while also getting the kids ready for the lantern parade … then everyone else knows that you may not be able to contribute a brilliant idea at the meeting today, and that is totally okay. I believe that this makes us all more human, and I like that a lot.

Now I am going to completely step out of my comfort zone

Several months ago, I had the opportunity to do a podcast on cancer. It was and continues to be important to me. I wanted to encourage others who had experienced similar or even worse diagnoses and tell them that there is no right or wrong way to carry this burden or a right or wrong way to try to beat the disease. I want to remove the taboos associated with cancer. And that is also a sort of therapy for me. It feels good to talk about it. I can make something positive out of my disease and my fate.

But I have never done anything like that before. I would even say about myself that I use rather simple language, and my grammar isn't the best. But I simply did it. If it had started to sound stupid or gotten really bad, I could have always quit doing it. But here again: I knew that there was a probability that it would be a success because I know what I can do. I have the self-confidence to stand up straight and say: "I am not a professional speaker, my 's' sounds too sharp, my grammar is not really good enough for such a podcast, but I also know that I am authentic, can draw people in, and am good at having a conversation."

So, I just tried it. And it worked. And it can work for you, too, even without having to go on such a painful learning experience first.

Here is my advice to you:

- Analyze what makes you truly happy and what satisfies you and prioritize that in your life
- Know your own strengths and weaknesses and work with them in a transparent way
- Don't be afraid to admit your strengths
- But also try to jump over your own shadow every now and then and work on your weaknesses
- Try to deliberately be imperfect
- Dare to go on new adventures without being the expert in that particular exploit
- Know that you are unique and fantastic
- Enjoy life

I believe in you and in all of us!

5. Formulate Statements, not questions

Let's move on to a very concrete situation: your regular business day. A couple of years ago, my team at Monster did a survey: Employees from different EU countries were asked how confident they felt in specific situations. No wonder – to ask for a pay raise was not the situation most participants, both women and men, felt comfortable with. But what surprised me was that raising your hand in a normal meeting and speaking up was also something people didn't feel confident enough to do[1]. I live by the motto: A meeting in which I haven't said anything is a meeting I shouldn't have attended at all. That so many people feel intimidated to speak came as a shock. Why? I am a very outspoken person by nature. So, talking and talking was never my problem. But I think that it was not only my tendency to be a loudmouth that gave me an above-average level of confidence to say what I want to say. I identified two other factors. First: I was lucky to work in teams which allowed people to give feedback regardless of their role or position. That helped me especially during the first years of my career. Second: I had brilliant managers who taught me how to survive the regular business drama of demanding bosses, uncooperative experts, and the constant battle about

---

[1] Monster's 2018 World of Work Study surveyed 5,072 participants in the UK, Germany, France, and the Netherlands (2,648 females, 2,424 male). 28% of the female and 21% of the male participants said they felt not very or not at all confident to speak up in a meeting. 31% of the female and 22% of the male participants said they felt not very or not at all confident to push for a new idea, 61% female and 45% male to ask for a pay raise, and 49% of females and 36% of males to go for a promotion.

*responsibility in meetings. One of them is **Elke Guhl**, a passionate marketing and digital transformation leader. I had the honor to work with her at Monster. She guided me through Business Communication 101. For this book, I asked her to share her tips on how to fight back nervousness when you are in a new team or face an opposition you don't expect.*

When I started my career in FMCG in the mid-90s, it was rare to find women in leadership positions – unfortunately today, despite all efforts, we are still not close to where we should be, but I guess this is a different topic for a different confidence commandment :) My first boss was a woman, and when I heard the news that she had died last year (quite young, in her early sixties), I realized just how much she had influenced my leadership style and business personality. She belonged to the generation of businesswomen who had to act or believed they had to act like a guy – tough, straight forward, demanding, distant, no emotions. It did not feel natural at all, it felt like a role she was playing. Sure, the team "followed" her, but nobody really liked her, we were all scared.

So, imagine being in your mid-twenties and entering a huge conference room for an advertising agency presentation of a new campaign – senior management positioned around the table, your boss sitting like a queen at the head of an impressive conference table, and you just sit down feeling overwhelmed by the scene and the "I-am-so-important" attitude of everybody attending this meeting.

When the agency finished the presentation, there was silence in the room. Nobody dared to say something – everybody was waiting for the words of our boss. And what did she do? She asked me to give my evaluation of the proposals presented, as the first one in the room. "Let's hear our Benjamin in the round first!" I don't remember what I said anymore, but I can still see this situation in front of my eyes. So, I tried to overcome my nervousness and gave my statement, then one by one, she asked everybody else for their opinion. She never commented on the statements. After listening to everybody, my boss gave her final personal statement, summed up and recommended the next steps for the agency. Boom. I was deeply impressed.

Over my first years in meetings with my boss, I learned some simple but important things:

- There is no right or wrong – there is only passion and confidence about a thought or opinion.
- Don't put questions marks in your statements – think always in exclamation marks!
- Every opinion or statement is valuable – even those from the youngest or least experienced team members or interns.

- Even more: The youngest team members have still the freshest and most non-political and un-biased view on things – this can be of huge help when making business decisions.
- Listening to statements of your team before you give your opinion as a team lead has a lot of advantages: Your team feels heard and respected, you have the time to reflect your view on things while listening to other opinions, and your final decision gets better buy-in when taking all views and opinions into consideration.
- When giving your opinion on something, always start with the positive feedback or facets. Spend time to celebrate, support, or appreciate. In case you criticize or disagree on things, always keep in mind to do it constructively and be solution-oriented – never be harsh or get personal or pretentious.

Moving on in my career, this experience gave me the trust to speak up, contribute my own reflections, and not to hold back. At the same time, it let me develop my own leadership style by respecting and grooming a team culture in which everybody is encouraged to actively speak up and bring in knowledge, opinions, and learnings – funny enough, this is a lesson that was taught by a boss who was not at all my role model in terms of leadership style or attitude.

"BUSINESS IS NOT ALWAYS ABOUT EXCHANGING OPINIONS OR STATEMENTS IN AGREEMENT – SOMETIMES, IT IS ABOUT POLITICS, PERSONAL INTERESTS, POWER PLAYS – LET'S NOT BE NAIVE HERE!"

But, obviously, business is not always about exchanging opinions or statements in agreement – sometimes, it is about politics, personal interests, power plays – let's not be naive here!

Especially when you a switching jobs and joining a new organization and team, you must be aware that you are entering an existing system with inherent rules, culture, behaviors, and roles, some of them not evident at first sight.

So, this is my second important advice to you: Before bulldozing into those new situations, it is important to listen first. Trying to understand personalities in your team, personal agendas, the communication culture, tonality, and the relations within in the team are key for your own communication. Using some time in the beginning to adjust to your new environment will prevent you from running into needless trouble.

And another piece of advice: Be aware of the fact that some colleagues want to test you as a new team member – they want to provoke you on purpose to see how you react and to determine the "ranking" or role you get in the team... sadly, I have experienced this mostly in male teams.

When I took a job in the USA as a Marketing Director (sent from my German Headquarters to the local unit), I had exactly this situation with my colleague, the Sales Director – he wanted to test me! One day, he wrote an email asking me for my action on a retail partner. As I wrote him back that I needed some more time to analyze the situation before coming back with a recommendation, he sent me the following mail in capital letters: "ELKE, WE ARE DROWNING AND YOU ARE CHECKING THE WATER TEMPERATURE! MOVE!"

Well, I moved – quickly downstairs to his office! How did he dare! An email like this! I stormed into his office. Our CEO who was in the office with the Sales Director stood up with the words "I'll better leave", and I stood face to face with our Sales Director. Very calmly and coolly (despite my heartbeat), I told him that I did not appreciate him sending mails like this but preferred a personal conversation. Which we then had. After this, life with him got much better because I had shown my self-confidence, did not hide, and not only went into the conflict but created a solution with him. Test passed! When I left the job two years later, he told me that he had worked with a lot of marketing people by then but had liked working with me the most – you surely can imagine my big fat grin.

In a nutshell:

1. Use the power of diverse opinions and listen to them to build your own opinion
2. Be clear and straightforward with your statements – put exclamation marks!
3. When providing feedback, always put the positive first
4. Understand the organizational culture and team rules & habits before speaking up
5. Be authentic and self-confident and do not take things too seriously
6. Understand power plays and cleverly take part
7. Don't shy away from conflicts – they can be quite catalytic and turn into positive endings

6. Eliminate distractions and do not hide behind them

*No one is a natural "confidence professional". If you are looking at the most-liked TED talk performances or speeches, you will see that what looks natural and easy-going is the result of a lot of preparation. Like we heard before – to come prepared and know your stuff is one element of speaking and leading with confidence. How long did you rehearse your presentation before your project group the last time? Ten minutes? Not at all? Ah, you hadn't had the time to prepare and get feedback. There had been the sorting of your mailbox (long overdue), the email to the supplier you never want to buy from, the article you absolutely needed to read. I understand, you are getting easily distracted. And this is hindering you from preparing, and this is leading to feeling guilty about not preparing, and this is leading to not feeling prepared at all, and this can only end in a disaster, so why not cancel the whole presentation or postpone it? Everyone will be happy to just read the written version. No, they will not. They should hear from you, on stage and in person. You need to stop hiding behind the distraction, because the distraction is only a symptom of your insecurity. Confidence comes with getting out of your comfort zone and doing it. My colleague **Roxanne Tashjian** is one of the best organized business partners I have had the pleasure to work with. I asked her how important preparation and planning is for her in her role as a leader and manager.*

"Anything worth doing is worth doing right"

This famous quote from Hunter S. Thompson resonates with me, and yet, distractions can often get in the way of success. It may seem obvious, but the key is *preparation.*

Think about a movie production... How many "takes" do you think there are to do a scene? Or how many tries does it take to create the "demo" video or personal Instagram photo? What if you are going into an interview... Do you just walk in without practicing first? I bet you do your research ahead of time and prepare to put the best version of yourself forward. (Hint: If you don't – you should!) The same should hold true for anything you deem important.

Being prepared as a leader ensures your work will go as planned, or if it goes in another direction, you can respond with ease. Great leaders spend time preparing and being proactive. They think about the future, plan and prepare for the unknown. Yet, it's easy to get caught up in day-to-day activities and to let things distract you. The key is to recognize the distractions and keep them at bay.

Are you thinking, "Sure, Roxanne, but how?" I'd like to share some tricks to help you be proactive and, specifically, how to prepare for a big event.

"I PREPARED, AND THEN PREPARED SOME MORE."

I am sure you've heard people say, "Get out of your comfort zone," so let me tell you a quick story. I used to tell people that myself, until a few years ago, when my team and I won a large award. We were so excited to win this award, and then I was told that I had to present at their annual conference on the main stage in front of 3,000 people for 40 minutes. At first, I thought this would be tough, but I'd have a monitor and notes, and I'd get through it. Then the second surprise: Oh, there is no monitor for notes. As panic set in, I realized instantly that I needed help. I thought, "How do the TED Talks people do this?" Yes, their talks are shorter, but still...I had to overcome my doubts and do it. But how?

I prepared, and then prepared some more. While planning, I realized a confidence monitor for this length of a talk was necessary, so I negotiated with the organization and they complied. (Bonus tip: Don't be afraid to ask for what you need!)

Here are some tips to help you stay on track:

Don't procrastinate
- This will just leave you with more anxiety and less time to prepare.

Prepare a reverse timeline
- When is the event?

Work backwards, see how much time you have, and plan each task from there

Develop your presentation
- Prepare an outline
- Develop your presentation
- Prepare your script

Get someone to review it with you and provide you with honest feedback
Practice, practice, practice
- It's important to not just learn your content but to practice: Where will you pause for impact? Make sure your delivery emphasizes the key words and pay attention to your body language. The amount of practice directly relates to your level of comfort on the content and level of expertise on your delivery. During practice, video yourself (or have someone help you), so you can review your stance, your talk

track, and your delivery, and adjust accordingly.

I practiced for hours for my big presentation. I rehearsed it while I was walking my dog or while I was getting ready in the morning, and I timed myself to see if I would finish within the allotted presentation time.

To be professional and to come across as knowledgeable, you need to prepare. Distractions always come up and other priorities come into play, so I recommend scheduling in a few extra rehearsals to cover yourself.

What about handling distractions on a daily basis?

One trick I find helpful to be proactive at work is to block my calendar at least one hour a day and to use this time to plan my day and my week or month ahead. You can also shut off your IM while working on a project so that you won't get interrupted or pick one or two times a day to answer emails. This helps me be proactive rather than reactive and helps me keep distractions at a minimum. Another tip I incorporate into each day is to get outside and go for a walk. This has proven to help inspire me with ideas. When I get back to my desk, I immediately put my thoughts down on paper if I haven't already recorded them on my phone while I was walking.

As a last tip, I just want to remind you that being prepared is not exclusive to an event or a task. I encourage you to make time to read articles and take the opportunity to learn whenever you can. Knowledge is power and gives you the confidence to be able to have a conversation about a variety of topics. Plus, filling your time with proactive activities also means there is less time for those pesky little distractions.

7. Use the power of 'no'

*Within a business environment, confidence comes with knowing your sh*t. How about that situation we all fear, when someone is throwing that big question at you, the one you are not able to answer? How do you react? With confidence or will you search for the hole in the floor telling yourself that your career will end now? It can happen in a meeting with two dozen colleagues eagerly waiting for your reply or in a one-on-one with your boss. Perhaps you are fresh in the role and just don't know everything yet. Doing stuff for the first time is a struggle. You are scared. Or you are not ready and prepared. Or it is just not your field. Or you thought that you were right, and now you realize that you might be wrong. I talk to my colleague **Louise Goodman**, marketing expert for over 15 years, a lot about these situations. Also, I talk to her about the option to say "No" and "Not now". But let her explain... and perhaps she also likes the quote from Sara Blakely, who said: "Don't be intimidated by what you don't know. That can be your greatest strength and ensure that you do things differently from everyone else."*

No – it's such a simple little word. Isn't it?

Saying 'no', whether it's to a boss who has more work for you or to a friend who wants you to go out, can feel impossible. Saying 'yes' is often seen as the easy option, but 'no' and 'yes' are always, in my view, inextricably linked.

Every time we say 'yes' to one thing, we're making a choice; we are saying 'no' to something else. If we take on that extra work that we don't have the capacity for, we are saying 'no' to going home at a reasonable hour or delivering other projects on time or to the standard we want to. If we accept the invite to the social event that we don't really want to go to, we are saying 'no' to a much-needed night in.

Saying 'no' is important, because it means that we're establishing boundaries for ourselves, it means that we're saying 'yes' to putting, or at least trying to put, ourselves first. And yet, it's something that still seems to fill us with fear.

I can't speak for anyone else, but I used to feel like I had two default settings; a blunt 'no' that always felt a bit rude or a bumblefest of excuses and apologies worthy of Hugh Grant, where it wasn't actually clear what I was trying to say.

Often, the issue was that I simply didn't have the confidence to have a constructive conversation, and a large part of that was the environment I was in. Before joining Monster, I spent 18 years working at advertising agencies. I learnt a lot and made some wonderful friends along the way; however, I almost always had more work than could reasonably fit into a working day. Having too much to do and working long hours was normal. Which meant that I had to learn a few creative ways to manage requests that I, or the teams I ran, rarely had the time to take on.

While there are some work situations where a straightforward 'no' is appropriate, and possibly unavoidable, quite often, just saying 'no' is not going to do us any favors. In these situations, we need to try to reframe the discussion in a way that allows us to voice our concerns and reservations and that acknowledges the constraints we're working under.

"SOMETIMES, THE POWER OF 'NO' IS REALLY ABOUT NOT SAYING 'YES' STRAIGHT AWAY."

I think that what we're really looking for in most of these situations is to feel heard and to feel like we have a choice, even if we can't ultimately change the outcome. Sometimes, the power of 'no' is really about not saying 'yes' straight away.

Here are a few things that I think can help us to use the power of 'no' effectively at work:

1. **Buy yourself time:** For example, "Let me get back to you on that" or "Let me have some time to think about this"

2. **Be positive:** For example, "That's a great idea, let's review it against what we're already working on" vs. "There's no way we can take that on at the moment"

3. **Offer solutions:** "We may have to make some tough decisions about what we can deliver on other projects to get it done but I have a few options to discuss with you"

4. **Don't be afraid to negotiate:** For example, "I can do X or Y by the end of next week so if you need both by then, I'll either need more resources to help with the workload or we'll need to review what's delivered by then. Let's discuss"

5. **Understand what's in it for you:** For example, make sure you know how this will help you achieve your goals, be that spending more time with your family, learning a new skill, or getting a promotion / pay raise.

Using the power of 'no' can help us have the confidence to have more constructive conversations about something that we can't or don't want to do. I think that being able to say 'no' without feeling guilty is a superpower, and one we all deserve to have.

8. Be confident on the outside and you will also become it on the inside

*You probably know the term „dress for success"? This regularly comes with a nice fashion selection of power suits and hairstyles. But before you roll your eyes and flip to the next chapter, let's acknowledge that the way you present yourself to others, by your personality and postures, movements, and the way you "own your space", does have an impact on how they see you. Believe me. I am a petite woman, and I know how important it is to make myself literally larger than I am. I started with little things and tried out different roles and styles before I found my confidence-personality. There are different ways and facets you can work on to start to show confidence on the outside even before you are feeling it on the inside. I talked to the communication expert **Larraine Solomon**, who trained and worked with a lot of C-level managers and asked about her secret tips for them and for you.*

"Whether you think you can, or you think you can't – you're right"

is among my favorite quotes. It suggests that your belief in your own abilities will determine your chances of success.

One of the things that I enjoy the most is working alongside smart people, and in my career, I have been very fortunate to have worked with leading scientists,

CEOs, entrepreneurs, politicians, and business leaders. In every role, I have enjoyed tapping into their technical knowledge, hearing their passion about a subject, and observing their leadership style. In spite of the fact that my knowledge of their expertise is usually very limited, my job is to add commercial value to them by giving them advice and sharing my experience-based skills. In an environment where they know far more than I ever will about their business and industry, self-assurance, coupled with a degree of tenacity, goes a long way.

"...BUT I HAVE TRAINED MY INNER VOICE."

A number of years ago, I did some work with a Paralympic athlete coach who triggered a light-bulb moment when he shared a simple and seemingly obvious concept. "When you are an elite athlete," he said, "being the fastest, strongest, or having the most endurance is rarely the biggest challenge. In fact, positive self-talk is one of the most difficult sports skills to master and can make the difference between a gold medal and no medal."

A soccer player who tells himself, "I missed my last penalty, and therefore I might miss this one," will need to practice replacing that negative thought with a more positive one: "I'm going to score this penalty" to win. With repetition and over time, an athlete can develop a new habit of thinking about positive outcomes, leading to an increased chance of succeeding. There is a direct connection between the voice in your head, self-belief, confidence, and scoring that penalty.

I have sat on many company boards, often as the least qualified and experienced person in the room when it comes to the topic on the agenda. I have also regularly been the only women in the meeting. When a colleague once asked me why I don't feel intimidated in these forums, I didn't need to think too hard about my response. "I bring critical expertise and experience in terms of communication, which is a unique skill that everyone in the room needs in order to succeed. I have seen what works and also what is less likely to work, and I bring a new perspective that will enable and enhance their leadership." Early in my career, I would have reacted with hesitation to that question, but I have trained my inner voice. One of the things that has grounded me is that almost always, when I have developed really trusted relationships with confident and successful senior leaders, I have discovered that they have the same fears and vulnerabilities that everyone else does.

My 6 tips for increased confidence on the inside as well as the outside

Focus on what goes right rather than unduly worrying about things that don't always go your way. I recently did some fascinating work with a neuroscience expert. She helped me to understand that we have an intrinsic instinct to minimize threats as quickly as possible and to a lesser extent in order to seek out the rewards. The threat instinct has a far greater impact on our brains than the latter. As an example, if an individual receives two emails, the first full of praise and the second critical of their work, in most cases, the critical email will create a lasting impression, as we are more sensitive to threats. By realizing this fact, you can positively change your response.

Pay it forward. Helping others to succeed by being generous with your time, knowledge, and experience is always worthwhile. Not only will this be personally fulfilling, but you will eventually surround yourself with colleagues that want you to succeed as well, providing a symbiotic confidence boost.

Develop and nurture a trusted support and challenge network. Keeping in touch with colleagues that you respect, can learn from, and have developed a close connection with is essential. Some of my most valued contacts have been people who have challenged my thinking, supported me when I needed it the most, introduced me to amazing people, and have even provided unique work opportunities.

Do something that scares you often. Deliberately stepping outside of your comfort zone is never easy but manage it well and it can provide a huge confidence boost. Don't be afraid to fail sometimes. In fact, there is a lot of research that talks about a place of "optimal anxiety" where your performance is enhanced dramatically, and that only happens when you get out of your comfort zone.

I'm a great fan of Daniel Pink, author of *Drive: The Surprising Truth About What Motivates Us.* His philosophy is: "If you're too comfortable, you're not productive. And if you're too uncomfortable, you're not productive. Like Goldilocks, we can't be too hot or too cold."

Always be curious. Think about a time when you started something new – a job, a hobby, or a new skill. Certain triggers led you there and sparked your curiosity enough to venture into new territory. Being curious tells us that it's okay to explore and be a beginner. It can shift the focus from your internal voice saying, "I might not be good/smart/capable enough…" to a less judgmental viewpoint of: "What might this be like?" or "How can I succeed?". Ultimately, relentless curiosity will enable lifelong learning – a powerful ally of self-confidence

Celebrate success and enjoy what you do. It's not just about the big wins, small successes are often important as well. Your energy is your brand, and the shadow that you cast will impact the way people feel about you, as well as how you feel about yourself.

Finally, if you are not a naturally confident person, remember that you are not alone. World-renowned Italian Renaissance artist Michelangelo doubted his abilities before he created his masterpiece fresco painting, The Last Judgment, in the Sistine Chapel.

In the early 1500s, Pope Julius II asked Michelangelo to paint the ceiling of the Vatican's famous Chapel. In response, Michelangelo refused, saying that he was a sculptor and not a painter. Eventually, he accepted the Pope's request and spent four years painting the chapel. Since then, it has been one of the most famous frescos in history!

9. Accept Compliments and give them to others often

During my working life, I found this one of the easiest and one of the hardest things to do. Are we trained or conditioned to downplay achievements with: "Oh, that was nothing, I actually didn't find myself that great" or, "That was not me, that was someone else"? You have done that recently? Me too. We do not accept a 'well done'. On the other hand, I am very generous with giving compliments to others. To say, 'Thank You' and 'Good Job' is for free, and it could mean the world to someone. For me, the concept of accepting and giving compliments is connected to self-acceptance and self-love. Two concepts that **Maren Hallin**, *my wingwoman at the job, knows a lot about. She is so kind to talk about her views.*

The other day, I came across a very simple but straight-to-the-point quote that has stuck with me ever since. It goes:

> **"When you are confident, people become confident in you."**

For me, it captures the essence of what it means to be confident. It so beautifully underlines that confidence is an "inside job", period.

Let's face it, confidence doesn't really come from what other people think of you, but from what you think about yourself. Only if you truly feel good about you and your doing, it will spill over to your surroundings, to your coworkers, to your boss, to your family, and everyone close to you. Interestingly enough, many women oftentimes still have the tendency to keep their self-confidence hidden rather than putting it on display, keep on downplaying rather than elevating it, and being okay with standing in the second row even though they belong at the front of the crowd.

Why? Because we have learned – especially as women – that modesty is a virtue, that too much self-confidence is perceived as cocky and that feeling proud might be mistaken for being big-headed. And actually, the way we treat compliments captures this tendency very clearly.

Think of the last time you were recognized and complimented for the work you have done. How did you react? Likely, you tried to brush it off with the words: "Oh, that was nothing", "This was a team effort", or a "Thanks, but I think I could have done better." I myself can't count the number of times I have used those phrases after I got a compliment about the work I delivered, the project I finished, or the presentation I held. Spoiler alert: If you see yourself in this as well, you and I are not the only ones. Nearly

70% of people associate embarrassment and discomfort with the process of being complimented or recognized and often try to avoid it all together, according to a study by Christopher Littlefield.

Giving compliments, on the other hand, is a whole different story. I absolutely love giving compliments. And the reason is simple: It takes no effort and can make a huge difference. And it usually feels pretty good! In my experience, a small "thank you" or a genuine "well done" has the power to elevate the connection to your counterpart and the atmosphere at work or in your private life in no time.

Well, guess what… Isn't it just as important to elevate the connection to ourselves? In the end, accepting a compliment with pride is the best opportunity to recognize yourself, to strengthen the connection with yourself, and to fuel your self-confidence. **Ask yourself: Do you love yourself enough to recognize yourself?** Think about it: Self-confidence is ultimately connected to self-love. According to the Merriam-Webster dictionary, "self-love" is defined as "an appreciation of one's own worth or virtue". Every compliment, given or received, does exactly that: Showing appreciation for one's doing and being. The more difficult part is the translation for it to become a recognition of oneself. And even if the answer to the above question is still not a crystal-clear one – it sure isn't for me sometimes – we can work on it with a step-by-step plan, so that we are ready and can make the most out of it when we are being complimented the next time:

Step #1: Hear it. First of all, when a compliment comes your way, give it space to be heard. Listen to it, pay attention to it and, most importantly, give the other person the chance to express it fully! Because any kind of compliment is a two-way street... You are usually not the only one in this equation. Give your counterpart the joy of giving the compliment and to build that positive connection.

Step #2: Accept it. No more downplaying... Instead of falling into the trap of relativization to appear modest, hold your head high and simply accept it. Say "thank you". That's it! And make sure you leave the "..., but" out of the sentence.

Step #3: Recognize it (and yourself). Yes, you just got a compliment! Not the person next to you, not the team, not your alter ego, it was you! Take a moment to let that sink in and recognize it fully. Recognize yourself by emphasizing and repeating to yourself: "Yes, I did a good job", "Yes, I nailed this presentation", and "Yes, I deserve this compliment". This might be the tricky part, but since you successfully delivered the task and were complimented for it, this too simply needs practice.

Step #4: Appreciate it. Finally, appreciate the compliment you received and the chance it gave you to connect to the other person and, most importantly, to yourself. This is the moment when you can practice self-love and can deposit it in your inner self-confidence bank account. And this usually comes with a pretty good interest rate!

"WITH EVERY COMPLIMENT WE RECEIVE AND WITH EVERY COMPLIMENT WE ACCEPT, WE CAN GROW SELF-CONFIDENCE FROM THE INSIDE"

The beauty of this is the realization that every compliment we give to others is an opportunity to learn and help the other person to work on the most important connection we have – the one to ourselves. With every compliment we receive and with every compliment we accept, we can grow self-confidence from the inside – the only place where it truly can prosper, develop and ultimately spill over to our environment and the people around us. And that's all we need to thrive and strive. You rock!

10. Make it about others

Purpose is one of the biggest drivers you can experience in your life. If you see the sense in something, you are willing to go the extra mile. You will be willing to explore the world outside your comfort zone and be confident.

*There is a woman that I admire for what she is doing for other women: **Natascha Hoffner**. She is the founder of herCareer, the biggest event for women and business in Germany. She is a role model for what you can achieve when you really want to do it.*

I have been passionately working exhibitions for over 20 years. I learned the art of the trade in a small Mannheim exhibition corporation, which was taken over by the Deutsche Messe AG at some point. I started as a trainee and made it to manager. But at some point, I reached my limits, especially due to my situation at home. When I had my first child, I was still commuting between my home and my work, from Mannheim to the Munich area, which was some 400 km. That was completely fine for my husband and me at the time, who took on the brunt of the parental work.

But when the second child arrived, it became clear that we had reached our limits with this approach. There was no way I could return to a manager position. But I absolutely did not want to leave my job, either. It was important to me to be independent from my husband – including financially. But it was also clear that I wanted to remain in the exhibition sector.

Start with the why

I experienced time and again that women were not taken seriously – especially on the management level – or that they didn't believe in themselves. Men, on the other hand, who often knew much less, could casually appear on the stage and could win over others much faster and with much greater ease. Due to my situation at home, I also knew that women are very interested in learning more about their career options, regardless of whether they are standing on the lower rungs of the career ladder or are already considered professionals or at the management level. Women make up 50 percent of the population but continue to be underrepresented in the important roles of the work force. The latest prognosis of the World Economic Forum states that it will take around 100 years until men and women are equal in professional terms. This must happen faster, and I aimed to increase the speed of that change – and continue to do so.

This is how the idea for my company started: I use the exhibition herCAREER to offer women, regardless of which stage of their career they find themselves in, a platform to exchange and network – across hierarchies. When I first started with my exhibition corporation, I wasn't afraid, even though I didn't have financial backup from a bank yet. My grit turned out to be worth it: I was fortunately backed quite quickly after that, when a regional bank called to let us know that our loan had been approved.

The power of networking

However: Success doesn't just come running along. The start already wasn't easy. I needed to find out what is necessary to even found a corporation, and I ardently wished for a network that could support me along the way. For years I had believed that I didn't have time to network. When I became self-employed, that radically changed. But I also suddenly realized this: I already had a small network from my previous work. Several service providers and partners immediately agreed to work with me when I told them about my idea to establish my own company. I could count on a basic level of trust.

Today, as founder of the exhibition herCAREER, I am in a constant exchange with employers and various organizations. I always keep my ears open in case I can connect someone from my network – not only as a potential employee, but also, for instance, as a speaker, a panelist, or an author. I am often asked by the media whether I know and can recommend experts on this or that topic. After interviews, which I hold in person, I also occasionally suggest other women who should be interviewed at some point.

A recommendation can also consist of introducing one woman to another at an event. Actually, we should allow ourselves to ask for that – I do this increasingly when I know that someone knows someone with whom I'd like to get in touch with. My experience is that, if we are introduced to each other by someone, we are perceived completely differently by our new acquaintance.

Role models: Giving others the spotlight

It is just amazing to see other women grow and to know that you were able to contribute to that a little bit. With herCAREER, I also have another goal: To make women more visible and to inspire them to step out of their comfort zone and into the spotlight themselves. "If we can see it, we can be it!" That means that role models provide new avenues of possibilities in our imagination – and, therefore, women's belief that they can make it to the manager's level or take on other jobs that require more responsibility.

Women free our oceans from plastics, they create aluminum-free deodorants, they recycle concrete, or work on technologies that can detect cancer more quickly. There are so many women who are creating something truly extraordinary. Many are actively involved in shaping our society. They want to affect change with their ideas and their visions – either by working at a company or as a founder, in politics, in science, or as a volunteer. Together with my team, I have repeatedly nominated extraordinary women for awards, such as the Emotion Award, the Edition F Award, or the German Start-up Awards, so that these women can become role models for other women or because they need to become more visible. They are examples that we need to put out there more.

"WE SHOULD OPEN DOORS WHEN WE HAVE THE OPPORTUNITY TO DO SO."

Sharing is caring

When creating the herCAREER community – online and in person – it was always important to me to give women the stage. That includes that they are ready to share their knowledge and experience. Sharing means caring. We have created a suite of formats for herCAREER that help women to enter the 'doing' phase. Meetups, talks, labs – those aren't traditional presentations, but provide the opportunity for interaction, during which the participants can discuss specific experiences, knowledge, and learning curves in small groups.

herCAREER is not only there to allow exhibitioners to present their products and services, but it is particularly important to us that the entire wealth of knowledge of persons and organizations is brought out into the open. When this is achieved, it is definitely worth all the work: I have already heard so many exciting stories at the exhibition. One speaker, for example, talked about how she developed an online business model without any prior IT skills, and what you need to consider when choosing an IT provider. One founder reported how she was able to elevate her company to the next level using artificial intelligence. Others have shared very practical advice, for instance, what a product specifications sheet is and what it requires.

Mutual trust as a foundation

We should open doors when we have the opportunity to do so – and without expecting something in return. If women don't empower each other, who will? A bad experience doesn't mean that everyone in a network is all about taking advantage of each other. Using envy and an elbow mentality merely hinder us along the way. We can advance only if we operate on a foundation of mutual trust.

Every single story that we hear from others can lead to us letting other women follow us or even pass us along the way. To me, this is true solidarity. It is not only us who grow in those moments, but everyone who enters into a connection through business or knowledge with others. We are able to achieve unbelievable things with our mutual support. Let's take the opportunity to become part of something bigger! To say it in the heart surgeon's words, Dilek Gürsory, about herCAREER: "I was surprised to find a network here that spans the entire country. A network that was built by women who are perfectly aware of their role in the professional world and who want to fulfill that role, each in her own way – with autonomy, confidence, intelligence, sensitivity, solidarity, and femininity. **And I was one of them just now.**"

Bonus

Bonus: Don't be scared of success

Don't be scared of success! A piece of advice you cannot take serious enough. Success is something that really can scare the sh*t out of you. Perhaps you have already had the experience that after the first high of a successful project has faded, fear takes over. Fear of not being able to repeat the success, fear that they (whoever 'they' might be) will find out that you haven't deserved the success in the first place, fear that others might not like you because they are not as successful as you are.

But you shouldn't fear success. You deserve it. Enjoy the feeling that you did something amazing while overcoming self-doubts and the nagging voice in your head that told you that it would not work out. You have proven it to yourself and to everyone around you.

How about turning a success into something else? Turn it into a "deposit" into your personal confidence account. Your confidence is a like a bank account – you are transferring experiences into it, and you earn interest over time. Every compliment you get, every "job well done", every "YESSSS, I did it" can be added to that account. Even if you are not a math genius, you can get a lot of profit out of it.

How about setting up a savings plan? You can do it by writing a diary – to document your achievements, by asking for external feedback – to see how others see you, by accepting compliments – to just be happy. Like any other savings plan, the magic doesn't happen overnight. You need to invest some time and effort. But it is worth it.

At the end of each month, you can review your confidence account. Look back on the previous weeks and enjoy how large your savings have become. Even in crisis years like 2020 and 2021, it is possible to start your confidence account. Your confidence team from this book will be the first to add something to it with a compliment: You are amazing!

The Confidence Blocklist

WHAT YOU COULD STOP NOW

Overthinking, being sorry, lying awake in bed reviewing yesterday's mistakes ... sound familiar to you? These are behaviors I experienced myself, and other women told me about them, too. They are all hurting your confidence and self-esteem.

Two years ago, I started to write my personal blocklist. The things I want to stop. The traps I do not want to fall into anymore. I wanted it to be easy and short. Something that I have on hand as a print poster on my office wall to remind myself. So far, it has helped a lot. And I have shared this list with my team and my friends. Now I want to share it with you[2]. Because it WORKS!

Break the habit!

1. Overthinking

2. People-pleasing

3. Inability to let go of defeats

4. Perfectionism

5. Apologizing

---

[2] Go to www.confidence-commandments.com/confidence-blocklist to download your copy.

Overthinking: Don't think too much and get wound up in "what ifs". Because then nothing gets done at all. Memorize this additional tip: Done is better than perfect.

People-pleasing: You cannot make it right for everyone. First, you must make it right for you. Afterwards, you can think of others. To fear that someone might not like you is real, but is it worth getting into a negative downward spiral because you want to be popular? Wouldn't it be good to know you are right and stand by your opinion?

Inability to let go of defeats: You made a mistake. Fine. Learn from it, try to not do it again and move on, girl. Confidence and self-esteem are built on making mistakes and trying things out. You cannot make an omelet without breaking some eggs.

Perfectionism: This is a big one for so many women I have had the pleasure to meet. It must be perfect ... always. But perfection takes time and is rarely achieved. Confident women know that you can also win with 80%.

Apologizing: "Sorry, perhaps I am wrong, ...". "Keep me honest here..." Stop, stop, stop saying sorry. Just delete it from your business vocabulary. How often do you hear a man starting a sentence with saying he is sorry? Correct, never. Don't make yourself and your opinion smaller than it is. Don't do that to your confidence.

These five ideas helped me a lot over the last years. I have used them in business meetings, taken them into consideration for emails, while I planned my day, and when I reviewed a project. Some might be easier to incorporate into your daily routine – start with those and add the others. You can also make them visible, e.g. as a print copy on your office desk, on your letterboard or in form of a mind map. I have mine as a postcard where I can see it every day.

To make them even more effective, you can find a partner and work with a colleague you like. Together, you can gently remind each other to follow the rules and what to stop.

But now, without any further ado, let's talk about the things you should start to do to build your confidence and develop your new **superpower**.

What we ask of you

What we ask of you

Thank you for staying with us until the end of this guide. We hope that you found some examples applicable to your life, especially for your professional life at work. What's next? Now is the time to put your learned lessons into practice because you are the one who will make a change: for yourself, but also for other women. You will be their role model, leading the change to more self-respect, self-awareness, and courage. Don't be shy, just do it.

That is what we, as your confidence squad, your team, are asking from you. We need you as a leader and as an example. We need you as our wingwoman. We need women who show other women that everything can happen if you really want it. That you can be successful and confident. That you can have an impact on others with confidence as your new superpower. A woman who has impacted the life of thousands of others with her self-esteem, who never holds back with her opinion, and whose political career I admire, is Katharina Schulze.

Katharina has been the chairwoman of the Parliamentary Group Alliance 90/The Greens and member of the Bavarian State Parliament since 2013. Her passion for politics, diversity, and equality for all has left a deep impression. Being now called one of the relevant faces of Germany's new political generation, she took the political stage by storm. She represents the idea to challenge the status quo and to do things differently. She decided to not accept an outdated perception of how a female politician should behave and act. In March 2021, she said in an interview with the German Mucbook blog[3]: "At some point, I decided that I would not become a compliant political robot because the world is too colorful and diverse and, with it, politics to allow myself to be squeezed into something like that." She says about herself that she has a strong, robust personality and that that has helped her to work with critical feedback and the way she presents her views with confidence. This is Katharina's final, inspiring statement for you!

"It's my honor to share my view at the end of this feminist book. I am convinced that, in times like these, it's time to move forward instead of just continuing as before. We are facing many challenges, and the current changes in the world demand innovative and courageous problem-solvers, new ideas, and new faces. We, women of the twenty-first century, have a role to play in this. Our society needs our knowledge, lived experiences and innovations so that we can shape our future. I want to invite you all to act more loudly and more progressively to cause disruptive change. We can

---

[3] Mucbook blog, 03-11-2021, by Carina Eckl;
https://www.mucbook.de/warum-muss-ich-mich-dafuer-verteidigen-dass-ich-fuer-etwas-brenne-interview-mit-katharina-schulze/

and need to work together and show solidarity to each other while tackling the many challenges ahead.

Someone once told me: Cold water won't be warmer if you jump later. So: Accept challenges and just try to address them! You have everything you need in yourself – and you will learn the rest on your journey. And, of course, you will make mistakes, but you will grow from them. You will meet wonderful people to ally with and fight for the good cause. And if you sometimes feel overwhelmed, stressed out, or ask yourself what you are doing – always remember: Many strong and amazing women have led the fight that got us here – it was never easy to change the system. So, it is our responsibility as well to pave the road for us and the next generation of women.

Keeping this in mind, I have been able to grow beyond myself several times in my career, learned a lot, and I am still happily on my way of making the world a better place – one step at a time."

Katharina Schulze

Chairwoman of the Parliamentary Group Alliance 90/The Greens.
Member of the Bavarian State Parliament since 2013.
Feminist since forever.

Acknowledgments

This book and the Confidence Commandments Project began as a crazy idea in a meeting room at the beginning of the COVID-19 pandemic. A simple LinkedIn post sparked a firework of ideas in a time when I was searching for confidence. They were the right ideas at the right time. Maren was there, listened to my brainstorming about a book and said: You should do it. I believe in you. And with that, I did.

First and foremost, I want to thank my experts – the wonderful, brilliant, intelligent, and compassionate women who invested their time to write down their stories for this book. Maren, Lou, Roxanne, Larraine, Natascha, Elke, Roxana, and Claudine, you have been so supportive and honest with your feedback. It was amazing to work with you. I was already impressed with you before the book, but now that I have read about your experiences and tips, I am all the more in awe. The women working with you in your teams or projects are lucky and will benefit from your guidance throughout their careers.

To Katharina Schulze for taking the time to contribute with an inspiring statement to give us some motivation for the future.

To my husband Markus, who is my rock. I wouldn't be who I am without him.

To my former managers and mentors, who helped me develop my personal confidence, guided me through the deep valleys of doubt, and encouraged me to use my communication talent to find my role. Elke, Sinead, Bernd, Claire and Marc – I am talking to you.

To the genius who said: **"Self-love is the greatest middle finger of all times"** for giving me a great motto for 2021.

To the readers – thanks for reading and for joining the network.

I hand over the torch of confidence to you. Now go out, spread the word, and be a wingwoman to every woman around you!

Thank you.

About the experts

Roxana Hughes

Plan for small-step victories

Roxana Hughes, currently working at Accenture, is a Marketing Enthusiast, hungry Lifelong Learner and Supporter of Confidence for everyone.

After layovers across Europa and North America, working at large corporations like Daimler, DB Schenker or Monster and futuristic start-ups like Tesla she gained great insights into modern business practice and into the various challenges ahead for companies and humans alike. With her passion for people, she loves helping people seeing their real potential. Currently, she lives near Stuttgart with the English husband.

Motto: If you don't ask, the answer is always 'no' #furturefavorsthebrave

Network with her or follow her on:

https://www.linkedin.com/in/roxanahughes

Claudine Petit:

Done is better than perfect

New Work Evangelist, Transformation Expert, Digital Pioneer, Tech Lover, Podcaster, Female Leader and Supporter, Cancer Survivor, Anti Cancer Activist, Mommy, Wify, Yogi, Design Enthusiast and huge fan of the Oktoberfest.

She is working as Lead transformation strategy at MSD, is the host, face and voice of the cancer podcast Café Krebs and home-based in Munich

Motto:

#Loveitchangeitorleaveit #gemeinsamsindwirstark

Her podcast: Café Krebs https://cafekrebs.de/

Insta: claudinepetit

Network with her or follow her on

https://www.linkedin.com/in/claudinepetit

Elke Guhl:

Formulate statements, not questions

Business Leader, Digital Enthusiast, Future Builder, Lecturer, Foresthugger, Mountainlover, Winesipper and Silly Mum.

Elke has worked and lived in Düsseldorf, Los Angeles, Basel and Frankfurt – and found her family home base in Zurich nearly eight years ago. Humbled to live in a city which feels like being in a constant vacation in a perfect global village.

Her heart is digital, and her soul is branding. She is driven to serve customer needs through relevant innovation by creating surprisingly valuable brand experiences.

Since 2020 Elke acts as Venture Builder in an exciting startup called **Brainforest** which started the purposeful journey to transform forest economy – have a look at brainforest.global

Network with her or follow her on

https://www.linkedin.com/in/elke-guhl

Roxanne Tashjian:

Eliminate distractions and do not hide behind them

Roxanne Tashjian is the Senior Vice President of Sales Effectiveness at Monster. She drives highly profitable organizational transformation, robust growth and energized teams.

Roxanne is known for building connections and cultures that drive organizational transformation in ways that bring everyone along on the same journey. She listens carefully and leaves no one behind.

A second generation American, Roxanne credits her strong Armenian upbringing for her independence and drive. She lives in Boston and her motto is **'treat all people how you would like to be treated and do not differentiate by level/role'**.

Network with her or follow her on

https://www.linkedin.com/in/roxanne-tashjian/

Louise Goodman:

Use the power of 'no'

Lou Goodman works for Monster as B2B and Product Marketing Director EU after almost 20 years working in agencies.

She lives in Bristol with her cat Freyja and loves travelling, cooking for friends and family, books, films, theatre and lazy days.

Motto: Let go of what you can't control

Network with her or follow her on

https://www.linkedin.com/in/louisegoodman/

Larraine Solomon:

Be confident on the outside and you will also become it on the inside

Larraine Solomon is the Managing Director of Inspiring Conversations Ltd, a UK based consultancy that helps organizations to deliver business success by making the world of work more engaging and productive for employees.

She is an executive coach, business mentor and a Trustee of a UK based charity. She lives in London and her motto is **'whether you think you can or think you can't, you're right'.**

Network with her or follow her on

https://www.linkedin.com/in/larraine-solomon-9270187/

Maren Hallin:

Accept compliments and give them to others often

Communicator, inspiration seeker, yoga student and teacher, Ayurveda enthusiast, motivator and change maker.

Maren lives in Frankfurt, Germany, and currently works as a Senior Marketing Manager for the job board Monster.de

Motto: Grow through what you go through.

Her love project is "anker mal" – it's all about Yoga, Ayurveda and finding the anchor in your life. Let's meet on the mat!

https://www.anker-mal.de/
https://www.instagram.com/anker_mal/

Network with her or follow her on

https://www.linkedin.com/in/marenhallin/

Natascha Hoffner:

Make it about others

Natascha Hoffner, Founder and CEO of herCAREER – the platform for female career planning.

Is the mastermind behind Germany's largest career platform for female career planning. Has 20 years of experience in the trade fair industry and founded messe.rocks GmbH in 2015. Doesn't want to accept that we won't achieve gender equality in the world of work for another 100 years, according to the World Economic Forum's forecast, and is doing everything she can to make it happen faster. Lives in Munich with her husband and two children.

Around the herCAREER exhibition, Natascha Hoffner has introduced numerous offers for networking and information for women: Experts' interviews, the herCAREER podcast and the digital herCAREER Jobmatch. She will soon be launching the herCAREER lunch dates for professional career exchange on topics such as starting a career, advancing to the next career level or founding a company.

Motto:

#strongertogether #machenistwiewollennurkrasser

Network with her or follow her numerous activities on LinkedIn

https://www.linkedin.com/in/nataschahoffner/
https://www.linkedin.com/company/11754675/
https://www.instagram.com/hercareer/
https://twitter.com/her_CAREER_de
https://www.facebook.com/herCAREER.de

Dr. Katrin Luzar:

Find a wingwoman & Do not compare compulsively

Storyteller, morning person, loves a good detective novel.

Supports women on their journey to confidence.

After finishing her doctoral thesis in communication science about "Content Analysis on the WWW" she worked for seven years at the PR agency fischerAppelt. In 2011 she joined the job board Monster.de as press secretary, took over the Marketing department in 2015 and became Senior Director Marketing EU in 2019 leading an international team. Her focus is brand management and content marketing. Her leadership style is collaborative and focuses on the power of sharing ideas and stories globally. Today she lives in Frankfurt, Germany.

Motto: "Hope is not a strategy"

Follow her and network on LinkedIn

https://www.linkedin.com/in/katrin-luzar-41047864/